Insects

الحشرات

By Katy Meeuwissen

Illustrated by Jovan Carl Segura

Please note, the two versions of this story have been written to be as close as possible. However, in some cases they differ to accommodate the nuances of each language.

برجاء ملاحظة أن نسختَي هذه القصة تمت كتابتهما لتكونا متقاربتين قدر الإمكان. لكن قد تكون هناك أحيانًا بعض الاختلافات لتناسب كل لغة.

Library For All Ltd.

A bee is an insect.

النحلة حشرة.

An ant is an insect.

النملة حشرة.

A beetle is an insect.

الخنفساء حشرة.

A fly is an insect.

الذبابة حشرة.

A mosquito is an insect.

الناموسة حشرة.

A butterfly is an insect.

الفراشة حشرة.

A moth is an insect.

العثة حشرة.

A flea is an insect.

البرغوث حشرة.

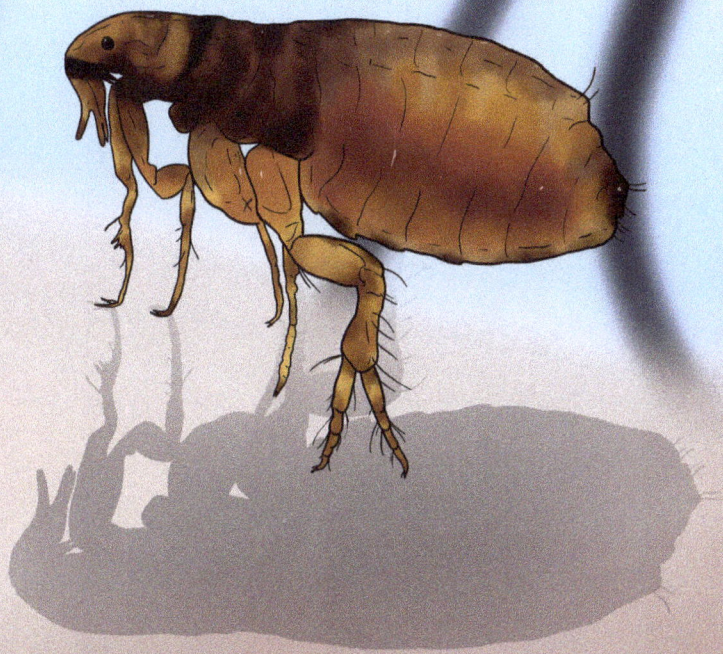

A dog is NOT an insect.

الكلب «ليس» حشرة.

Neither am I!

ولا أنا!

You can use these questions to talk about this book with your family, friends and teachers.

What did you learn from this book?

Describe this book in one word. Funny? Scary? Colourful? Interesting?

How did this book make you feel when you finished reading it?

What was your favourite part of this book?

Download the Library For All Reader app from librayforall.org

About the author

Katy Meeuwissen is a teacher who specialises in Early Childhood and primary education, working in the ACT directorate. Katy is currently working at the University of Canberra, teaching people to become teachers. Katy loves to teach children to read, write, learn and play.

Did you enjoy this book?

We have hundreds more expertly curated original stories to choose from.

We work in partnership with authors, educators, cultural advisors, governments and NGOs to bring the joy of reading to children everywhere.

Did you know?

We create global impact in these fields by embracing the United Nations Sustainable Development Goals.

libraryforall.org

Published by Library For All Ltd
Email: info@libraryforall.org
URL: libraryforall.org

Original illustrations by Jovan Carl Segura

Insects
Meeuwissen, Katy
ISBN: 978-1-923207-03-5
SKU04365

www.ingramcontent.com/pod-product-compliance
Lightning Source LLC
Chambersburg PA
CBHW042347040426
42448CB00019B/3438